PEUGEOT
205 GTI

MATTHEW CORRIGAN

AMBERLEY

First published 2020

Amberley Publishing
The Hill, Stroud,
Gloucestershire, GL5 4EP

www.amberley-books.com

ISBN: 978 1 4456 6528 3 (print)
ISBN: 978 1 4456 6529 0 (ebook)

British Library Cataloguing in Publication Data.
A catalogue record for this book is available from the British Library.

Typeset in 10pt on 13pt Celeste.
Typesetting by Aura Technology and Software Services, India.
Printed in the UK.

Contents

Introduction

For the Peugeot car company, the 205 hatchback was never conceived to be legendary. Yet in GTI specification with either the 1.6 or 1.9 litre power plant, legendary is exactly what it became. The word iconic is all-too-often bandied around, but for this diminutive French hot hatchback it is entirely appropriate. When Peugeot launched the 205 GTI they unwittingly gave the world a benchmark. Long after the factory ceased production and the model had been superseded, the motoring press would greet the arrival of every new example of the genre with the same, tentative, hopeful question: could this one be the new 205 GTI?

The Peugeot 205 GTI.

There really is no such thing as an overnight success. Building a legend takes time. This book tells the story of the Peugeot 205 GTI. When, where and why it was born, who were the personalities involved with its creation and how it went on to become what many believe to be the best example of its kind.

Chapter One

Beginnings

Thanks to their ubiquity, it is difficult to imagine a time when hatchback cars were a rarity. Britain's roads in the mid-seventies were, however, a very different place. The three-box saloon car was still very much king. Cars like Ford's Cortina and Escort dominated, along with models such as the Morris Marina, Austin Allegro and others from a profusion of different manufacturers, many of which have long since disappeared from the automotive planet. Even the Morris Minor was still an everyday feature, a visible link to a long-lost motoring past. Japanese manufacturers, having established a foothold, were starting to gain in popularity, thanks in no small part to their perceived (and actual) reliability. Yet they, too, were mainly producing booted saloons for the UK market. The Peugeot brand, if it registered at all, was known mainly for its 504. In saloon or cavernous estate form, the 504 was renowned for its smooth, Jaguar-like ride and hewn-from-rock engineering (indeed, they can still be found in use in parts of Africa, where they perform with aplomb on roads that would seem better suited to 4x4s). It was not, however, a particularly common marque.

It wasn't until the end of that decade that things really began to change. An increasing number of families were able to afford a second car. Often, this would be a smaller vehicle, perhaps cheaper to buy and run than the typical four-door sedan. Seeing the opportunity, car makers began to respond and the marketplace started to fill up. In just a few short years the sector established itself as an important sales generator. It wasn't the only change taking place. In a brave move, Ford announced a radical departure in its replacement for the ubiquitous Cortina. Eventually launched in 1982, the Sierra paved the way for a completely different style. Though Ford was maligned at the start, the company persevered, and it was soon clear that a more radical design language was going to be acceptable to the buying public.

For Peugeot, these were difficult years. With a dated range and a somewhat staid image, it needed a fresh competitor in the burgeoning hatchback market. Thanks to their chic little 5 supermini, staunch local rivals Renault had the bestselling car in France. Across the Continent, the Ford Fiesta, Fiat Uno and Volkswagen Golf ranges were proving highly popular. Peugeot's presence was maintained by the 104, a car that had started life as a four-door saloon with a separate boot. Although not a bad car to drive, its styling was rather dated. Several mid-cycle facelifts had failed to overcome this problem. Peugeot knew an entirely new model was required: with three and five-door variants, it must be modern,

Above and below: The Peugeot 104, seen here in five-door 'S' trim. Although the model was facelifted several times during its production run, it was clear that the Paolo Martin design was in danger of looking staid and out of date against the competition.

compact and desirable enough to make an immediate impact on the sales charts. Enter visionary car designer Gérard Welter, Design Director at Peugeot, with what was known internally as Project M24.

Initially, two design studies were considered. The feted Pininfarina SpA studios looked to Peugeot's past, presenting a concept that drew heavily on the straight-lined designs of the company's existing family, notably the large 505 saloon and the aforementioned 104. Welter's team, however, followed a different stylistic road. Their 'softer' design called for a more rounded shape, less reliant on the angular steelwork that had gone before. The management agreed. The in-house team was selected instead of the Italian coachbuilder and the final design was agreed in 1980, the first birth pangs of what would become the 205.

The pressure must have been intense. Project M24 was very much make or break and the fate of thousands of PSA Group workers hung in the balance. The car had to be a success. According to French automotive writer and biographer of Welter, Christophe Bonnaud, the designer was approached in the workshop one evening by Peugeot's then Commercial Director Jean Boillot. 'Gérard,' he said, taking the man into his confidence. 'Si nous ne reussissons pas cette voiture, nous somme morts' – 'if we are not successful with this car, we are dead'.

Having built their reputation on producing refined cars that rode well, Peugeot's management were determined that the 205, despite its diminutive size, would continue to uphold the standards they had set. Safety, too, was becoming an important (and marketable)

Gérard Welter.

8

consideration for manufacturers, and matters of fuel economy were, of course, an ever-present concern. What was needed was a body that was both lightweight and strong, a car that performed as well in a crash as it would on the road.

Computer Aided Design (CAD) played an important role in the development of the 205's shell. Although its steps could be traced back to the mid-sixties, when Dr Patrick Hanratty first began using software to automate processes at General Motors, the science was still coming into its own. Peugeot's CAD operators were able to establish exactly where the gains could be made in this respect, hugely speeding up the research process. The resulting bodyshell was an inherently rigid design. Tough enough to give the car a long life while – crucially – carrying no unnecessary weight.

At 2,418 mm the wheelbase of the 205 mirrored that of the 104 but the track – the distance between two wheels on the same axle – was considerably wider. This increase was to give greatly enhanced road-holding qualities. Front suspension was MacPherson Strut with an anti-roll bar mounted behind the wheel line. At the back, a torsion bar system was in place, with a specially developed rear anti-roll bar used on the higher-power models. This compact set-up allowed for relatively narrow rear wheel arches, helping to increase available space inside the car.

Several engine options were available from the outset. Peugeot carried over some of the smaller power units from the 104. The 'X' or 'Douvrin' engine – known as the suitcase engine due to the way it was mounted virtually on its side, requiring it to be split apart from the transmission for maintenance – was lightweight and reliable. With a 954 cc displacement, the base model produced 44 bhp. 1.1 (1,124 cc) and 1.4 (1,360 cc) litre units made 49 and 59 bhp respectively, with the latter powerplant achieving 69 bhp in the range-topping GT model. All were four-cylinder units with the gearbox mounted beneath. Unusually for the time, Peugeot chose to include a diesel option. By offering the 1.9 (1,905 cc) XUD9 engine that was already in use in the 305 range, Peugeot became one of the first companies to bring diesel power to the supermini class. The large physical size of the XUD9, with its more conventional end-mounted gearbox arrangement, demonstrated the versatility of the 205 shell and paved the way for what was to come.

For the European launch of the 205, Peugeot took the rather unusual step of debuting the car outside the Continent, heading instead to Morocco. In another marketing decision that told the world's press that things were about to be different, they choose to launch the five-door version ahead of its three-door sister. Ordinarily, due to the styling compromises necessitated by packaging, five-door hatches do not have the aesthetic appeal of their smaller siblings. Not so for the 205; it exuded style from all angles.

From the low bonnet line to the steeply raked rear screen, the car almost had the look of a coupe. Its svelte lines gave it class-leading aerodynamics, with a drag coefficient of Cd 0.34. Markedly different to its more angular competitors, the 205 perfectly encapsulated the look that was about to become the height of fashion. It epitomised the design-led style that would define the 1980s. Debuting what would become the new 'family' look, the rampant lion on the nose adorned a body-coloured grille.

Inside, the 205 was a revelation. Renowned designer Paul Bracq, who had worked for Mercedes-Benz, BMW and had even played a role in the design of France's iconic TGV trains, created a light and airy cabin. Narrow A and B pillars gave excellent all-round

Above, below and opposite above: Looking good from every angle. The inherent rightness of the design was obvious from the start. (Picture: Red car, Jonathan Miller)

The flat boot floor and split folding rear seats allowed for a large carrying capacity.

By placing the spare wheel in a cage mounted beneath the body, Peugeot further increased the 205's boot space.

visibility and a real sense of space. The seats were supportive and comfortable, and allowed for an almost perfect driving position. By mounting the spare wheel inside a cage beneath the rear of the car, it had been possible to give the car a spacious luggage compartment. The split rear seats could be folded almost flat, increasing the available boot space considerably.

On paper, at least, it all added up. With its wheel-at-each-corner stance, the 205 was compact and purposeful with an inherent Gallic charm. It was immediately clear that in terms of out-and-out kerb appeal, Peugeot had a winner. Welter's team had certainly got the looks right, but the journalists were all asking themselves the same question: how does the all-new car drive?

If Peugeot had any concerns, they were soon forgotten. The 205 was an almost instant hit. Although it lost out to the rival Fiat Uno in the 1983 European Car of the Year Competition, it picked up the British magazine *What Car*'s 1984 Car of the Year award and would ultimately go on to be named as Car of the Decade by the influential *Car* magazine in 1990. The 205 success story had begun.

In 1983, Ian Kirkwood was at the start of what would become a long career with Peugeot in the UK. At the time he was a parts manager for long-established Manchester dealership Tom Garner. More than most, he understood how important the new car would be for the company.

Above and overleaf spread: Timeless style. The Peugeot 205 is still a common sight on French roads. These photographs of 205s in general use were taken in Brittany during the summer of 2019 – testament to the longevity of both the design team's vision and mechanical resilience of the car.

15

'Put simply,' he said, 'It was make or break. If the car hadn't been a success, the company would have gone under.'

He summed up the 205's impact in one crisp sentence: 'It was a brilliant success: right car, right time, right from the get-go.'

Gérard Welter began work at Peugeot at the age of seventeen. He would remain there for forty-seven prolific years, rising through the ranks to become Head of Exterior Styling in 1975 and ultimately director of the brand's style some twenty-three years later. Alongside his work there, he forged a career in motorsport. Welter's racing cars became a regular feature at Le Mans. In 1988, French driver Roger Dorchy achieved a record high speed of 405 km/h at the Mulsanne Straight in a Welter-designed, Peugeot-powered WM P88. The record is unlikely to be beaten thanks to the addition of FIA-mandated chicanes two years later. Welter's last work for Peugeot was the RC-Z Coupe, but the 205 was always his greatest success. Gérard Welter died on 31 January 2018 at the age of seventy-five.

A rare picture of the 205's legendary designer, Gérard Welter, at home with youngest daughter Nastasia, who adored her father. (Family photos kindly provided by Rachel Royer, Monsieur Welter's widow)

Gérard and
Rachel.

Gérard Welter.

CHAPTER TWO

GTI

While the hatchback market was growing, another sector had all but disappeared. Aside from high-priced exotica (even a Porsche 911 was a relatively rare sight on Britain's roads at the time), the sports car was vanishing. The troubled Triumph TR7 finally ceased production at the start of the 1980s, as, at last, did the MGB. Anyone wanting a more sporting drive found their choices were narrowing. Ford persevered with its Capri (which would in fact soldier on until 1987) but it was undoubtedly dated and suffering from an out-of-date image. Beset with rust problems, the Fiat X/19 was never a huge seller in the UK, leaving offerings from lower-volume manufacturers such as Alfa Romeo or Lancia the only option. Sports cars were often seen as unreliable; their drivers almost expected them to break.

Contrary to popular belief, Volkswagen was not the first company to fit a hatchback car with a relatively powerful engine. BMW, Chrysler and even Vauxhall had beaten them to it. The Golf GTI was, however, the first to appeal to a broad audience. Fast, reliable and, thanks to its clean Giugaro-designed looks, aspirational, the Golf GTI had been born when a group of company engineers famously experimented by marrying an Audi 1.6 engine with Bosch fuel injection. The resulting car received its public debut at the prestigious Frankfurt Motor Show in 1975, firing the first salvo in what would become open warfare between manufacturers for at least the next decade and a half. The 'hot hatch' revolution was underway.

In 1980, Ford debuted the third generation of its class-leading Escort. Radically different from what had gone before, the Mk 3 Escort dropped the front engine/rear drive configuration that had been in place since 1968. Breaking with the convention, which had seen previous Escorts rack up win after win in rallying (which, thanks to Ford's superb marketing, translated into sales), the new car had a transverse-mounted engine and front wheel drive. Crucially, the Escort was no longer a booted saloon, instead adopting the two-box configuration for the first time in its history. With more than a decade of motorsport success to fall back on, it was only natural that a 'sporty' version of the car would be offered – Ford could see the success of the Golf GTI. The Escort XR3 appeared in September 1980 and clearly had the Volkswagen in its sights. A 1.6 CVH power plant provided the go, but it had become patently obvious that a key ingredient in the success or otherwise of a hot hatchback was very much the show. The XR3 rode on eye-catching alloy wheels and sported body-coloured bumpers. A set of driving lights added to the ensemble with a large rubberised boot spoiler the icing on the cake. Inside, sports seats and a two-spoke steering wheel created just the right ambience for the young family customers

Ford was aiming to attract. It was the first real attempt to knock the Volkswagen off its perch. It would not be the last.

Peugeot had dipped a tentative toe into the sporting hatchback market with the 104ZS, but with dated styling and just 66 bhp it was no longer a contender. It had always been intended to produce a high-performance version of the 205, a 'halo' model to top the range. What nobody outside the company had envisaged was just how successful an entrant the 205 GTI would be.

By fortuitous coincidence, a recent and far-reaching change in the world of motorsport was helping to boost the visibility of the 205. In 1982 the *Federation International d'Automobile* (FIA), the world's governing body of motorsport, introduced a huge change to the rallying regulations. By creating a new class, Group B, the FIA transformed the sport into a worldwide spectacle almost overnight. Previously, manufacturers entering either Group 4 or 5 had been required to produce 400 examples of the cars they wished to race. Group B merged them and halved the necessary number, effectively handing carte blanche to manufacturers to build the wildest rally cars ever seen. Group B cars employed high-tech and lightweight materials and were closer to Formula 1 racers than the road cars whose silhouettes they often shared. The adage 'Win on Sunday, Sell on Monday' was never truer and car makers flocked to the sport as its popularity soared.

Peugeot had seen the opportunity and was busily developing its own project to compete under the new rules: M24 Rally. With the marketing opportunities obvious, it was essential that the car should closely resemble the 205. Under the guidance of Jean Todt, the Peugeot Talbot Sport Team was born, and their new rally car was unveiled to the press. Sitting alongside a standard five-door 205 outside Peugeot's Paris offices, the similarities were undoubtedly there. Behind the wide wheel arches, air intakes, bonnet scoop and spoilers, the family DNA was easily discernible. Underneath the skin though, the story was very different.

The road ahead. A 205 GTI about to set out along the notorious A57 Snake Pass.

The rally car had a wider track and extended wheelbase. Where there might have been a rear bench seat, a 1.8 litre four-cylinder sixteen-valve turbocharged engine provided drive for all four wheels. As per the rules, 200 road-going versions of the car were built and the name with which it was christened would become iconic. The Peugeot 205 T16 was ready to go.

Above: Peugeot 205 Turbo 16. Ian Kirkwood's immaculate example photographed in its natural environment. *Below and opposite above:* The road-going version of Peugeot's unstoppable Group B rally car.

Above and overleaf: The T16 in rally guise. (Photographs courtesy of Koen Marcelis)

By the time the 205 GTI was ready for launch, the marketplace had become quite crowded. As if mirroring the Cold War that still provided an ominous backdrop to the period, an arms race was under way. Ford had added Bosch Jetronic fuel injection, enabling it to append that intensely desirable vowel to the boot lid of what was now the Escort XR3i. It had been joined by a hotter Fiesta, the XR2, giving the company another bite at the lucrative cherry. Volkswagen had increased the capacity of the Golf GTI to 1.8 litres and in September 1983 launched the larger and more refined Mk 2 version. The hot hatch was coming of age. Myriad other manufacturers joined the rush and enjoyed (or otherwise)

A consignment of right-hand-drive 205 GTIs lines up like an invading army on the Calais docks, ready to cross the Channel. This picture was taken in April/May 1984 by a twelve-year-old Jeremy Philips. Now Group Marketing Manager for the Hawkins Motor Company in Cornwall, he recalls being struck by the sight while on a school trip. It was the first time he had seen the 205, let alone the GTI. He immediately realised he was seeing something special.

varying degrees of success: the Renault 5 Turbo and Vauxhall's Astra (Opel Kadett) GTE proved to be popular additions to the genre while many others fell by the wayside. The Golf, however, remained king of the hill. Prior to 1984, no challenger had been able to lay claim to its crown.

The 205 GTI finally broke cover in southern Spain and it was clear from the outset that the car was a looker. Shorn of its rear doors, the 205 took on a more purposeful look. Styling cues from the T16 added to the allure. At the front end, driving lights were recessed within a deep front spoiler. The extended wheel arches were filled by a set of Speedline 14-in. alloy wheels shod with wide, low-profile Michelin tyres. A waist-high body strip in grey plastic continued the bumper line all the way around the car, with red piping emphasising the sporty feel. Pop-open rear windows provided ventilation for back seat passengers. The broad C-pillar bore black and red 205 GTI badges and the ensemble was completed by a subtle roof spoiler and deep rear under-tray beneath the bumper. Even standing still, the car signalled its intent. The designers had pulled off the difficult trick of making the GTI catch the eye while avoiding some of the brasher elements that had started to afflict the genre. It was very much of its time, yet subtle enough to retain the charm of the base model that had so captured the public's imagination.

Above and below: A later 1.9 GTI finished in red.

Thanks to Peugeot's determination to ensure the 205 rode as well as its customers had come to expect, the chassis had already been praised for both ride and handling. The GTI built on the foundations established by the base model. Firmer suspension components and strengthened mounting points took care of body roll and helped the already crisp handling to deal with the increase in power.

Above, below and overleaf: Photographed at the 2019 Peugeot Festival, this lovely early 1987 Alpine White 1.9 is owned by Peugeot Sport Club members Kevin and Nicola Jones.

Above, below and overleaf above: This silver car has been given a set of continental-style yellow driving lamps and customised with a grille stripe in Peugeot Talbot Sport colours.

Above and opposite: A 1990 1.9 GTI in black, catching the sunlight.

29

Above, below and opposite: First registered in June 1991, this Graphite Grey 1.6 GTI was a Peugeot company car. It underwent a restoration in 2015 and is now in frequent use.

Inside, bolstered sports seats held the driver and front seat passenger firmly in place. Black and red upholstery throughout reflected the car's sporting ambitions and, *de riguer* in any 1980s hot hatch, a bright red carpet lined the floorpan. Additional dials provided oil pressure and temperature information alongside the Veglia rev counter and speedometer.

Under the bonnet, the all-alloy 1.6 litre XU5J engine was transversely mounted and canted 30 degrees rearwards to help weight distribution. First used in the 305, the high-compression eight-valve, four-cylinder OHC unit was, for this application, fitted with Bosch Multipoint L-Jetronic fuel injection and tuned to produce 105 bhp and 99 lb/ft of torque at a peak 4,000 rpm. Noise, Vibration and Harshness (NVH) levels were kept under control thanks to the use of hydro-elastic engine mounts. A five-speed close-ratio gearbox was mated, as in the GTI's diesel sister, to the end of the engine, driving the front wheels through equal-length driveshafts. On paper, the 1.6 GTI was not as powerful as the Mk 2 Golf's larger capacity 1.8, but with an unladen weight of just 850 kg the Peugeot was more than 200 kg lighter. All the ingredients were in place to make a very quick car indeed. The VW was very much in the crosshairs.

Initial reports were highly positive. The GTI's handling wasn't just good, it was a revelation that redefined expectations. The engine was described as 'sparkling'. With a top speed of around the 120-mph mark and a respectable 0–60 time of 9.7 seconds, the car was pitched at the upper end of the hot hatch league. Statistics, however, only told part of the story. Peugeot hadn't so much made a fast hatchback as a sports car in more

A tight squeeze under the bonnet of a 205 GTI. The XU5 engine and ancillaries.

practical clothes. When *What Car* magazine pitted the GTI in a back-to-back test with Ford's XR3i and (as was) the BL Group's MG Metro it won hands down in every respect. In simple terms the 205 GTI steered, handled and outpaced the competition in real world conditions. Volkswagen, at last, had a serious rival. Worryingly for the Germans, the 205 GTI was launched with a list price of just £6,245. By delving deeply into the parts bins of the various marques that made up the group, PSA had been able to keep a tight lid on development costs. The new car undercut the rival Golf by an incredible £1,600.

Chapter Three

First Thoughts

Four miles to the south and west of Buxton, a tiny village nestles in the moorlands at the extreme north end of Staffordshire. Clinging to the southern slope of Axe Edge Moor, it claims, at 463 metres above sea level, to be the highest village in Great Britain. This was not, however, the principal reason it was used as the starting point for a 2,000-mile road test to be undertaken by *Car* Magazine. The journalists who set out aboard a pre-production 205 GTI in 1984 chose the location simply because it had an interesting name. As it turned out, that name was rather appropriate to the subject matter at hand: flash.

Wearing an A-prefix registration plate, their 500-mile example was one of just two 205 GTIs in the UK at the time. As the seasoned road testers lowered themselves into the hip-hugging seats, Peugeot's press people would have been forgiven a degree of trepidation. Ronald 'Steady' Barker, Ian Fraser and the notoriously demanding L. J. K. Setright were not known for pulling their punches. This would be a hugely important test.

Nobody has ever made the perfect car and of course they found faults, not least with an undulating quality to the car's ride which had, in fairness, already been admitted by Peugeot engineers (work was already underway to address the apparent flaw). Praise, though, far outweighed any criticism. All of them would write with enthusiasm about the car's terrific road-holding, gear change and willing engine. Refinement, too, was singled out, the car's smooth shape working to ensure wind noise was kept to a minimum. The driving position was questioned, with the suggestion that taller (over 6 foot) drivers might find themselves sitting too high in the seats and there were minor niggles about instrument positions and noise from the heater fan. On the whole, though, the little Peugeot impressed, its sheer driveability winning them over:

And the handling! The compactness and the balance of the car combine with the stickability of the 60-series tyres to give the 205 GTI that brand of handling you experience only in the likes of a Fiat X1/9: you know that whatever the characteristics of the corner that's approaching, the car can cope. It seems able to widen any corner, there's a terrific amount of roadholding available, and the chassis is tuned for a tingle of throttle-off oversteer, the most stable kind. In fact, the car's tendency to tighten its line in corners is delicately variable, according to the amount of engine braking you apply through the admirably throttle-sensitive engine. If there's a criticism, it's the way the rack and pinion steering (3.8 turns, lock to lock) loads up under maximum effort cornering. The sharpness never varies, for all that.

The car's A-roads speed and passing ability relies on this any-situation competence (there's really not much understeer even in the tightest bends, taken with rubber-peeling ferocity) as well as on the strength of the engine, when delivered through those top three, close ratios. It's a joy to drive fast, this car; one particular dash from Norwich to Birmingham, some of it on saturated roads, a lot of it around lumbering camions, will live in my memory. To do it significantly faster, I'd have to have been on a motorcycle, and a good one.

Only L. J. K. Setright, who had previously gone on the record to state his belief that Peugeot should return to producing the kind of loping-gait saloons for which it had been previously been known, struck a dissenting note. He did, however, single out the 'delightfully light' feel of the GTI and its 'unbelievably sweet gearchange.'

Famously – or was it infamously – Setright had cast his vote for the Italian hatchback to deprive the 205 of the European Car of the Year Award. Upon driving the GTI, his first comments alluded to that decision.

Setright has become notorious for failing to see why everybody else should be so wildly enthusiastic about the Peugeot 205. Driving a disguised prototype 205 GTI last September strengthened his dissidence, but the production version alters the picture.

For instance this was the first 205, of six sampled, to make no wind noise. The body is now evidently as smooth as it looks (despite the visibly poor fit of the trim around the wheel arches), and its low drag must account for the brilliant upper-range acceleration. Lots of little whizzbangs may manage 0–60mph as fast as the Peugeot, though few can feel so delightfully light, but 0–100mph in 23 sec is surely exceptional.

This lightness is one of the greatest virtues of the 205. Another is that unbelievably sweet gearchange, a Peugeot speciality.

His colleagues, perhaps more accepting of what Peugeot had set out to create, didn't need to preclude their thoughts with such disclaimers, and penned the following comments:

Ronald Barker:

In three words this liveliest and most adventurous Peugeot product feels Right First Time. I didn't find a press colleague who wouldn't be glad to own one...

The Peugeot has all the dynamic assets for rating in the best company; a most pleasing blend of tenacity, balanced control, braking and ride comfort. The tyre grip is not too much for ordinary drivers like you and me, and the overall behaviour flatters our abilities. If you can think of a car in terms of average speed potential over second-grade roads rather than those stereotype figures on the spec sheet, the 205 GTI becomes truly formidable. Its compact size and sharp response are ideal for that.

Ian Fraser:

Finding successors to the revered Mini Coopers has been a stumbling affair finally given respectability by the Golf GTI during the '70s, the initially badly botched Escort XR3 in the early '80s and now by the Peugeot 205 GTI which has mostly avoided everyone else's errors.

What Peugeot have done is to create a separate model, properly styled, properly developed and properly in the mould of the rapidly changing mid-'80s. It has also reaffirmed Peugeot's position as top-echelon makers capable of turning out forefront cars of integrity.

Well aware of potential shortcomings in the car's rear suspension set-up, Peugeot's engineers were working to rectify the problems. Revisions were already being planned and would soon make their way into production. The opinions of the *Car* magazine journalists were held in very high regard and would be incredibly important to the UK sales campaign. The 205 GTI had passed an important test.

The first GTIs went on sale in April 1984. Buyers were able to choose from five colours: Alpine White, Cherry Red, Graphite Grey, Silver or Black. Early cars suffered from the ride problems identified by the *Car* journalists and in February the following year, following customer feedback, Peugeot revised the spring and damper rates to give the GTI a softer ride.

In its 18 May 1985 issue, *Motor* magazine printed the results of its own long-term test under the heading 'Affordable Excitement'. Throughout the previous year its testers had put nearly 25,000 miles on a 205 GTI, exposing it to a wide range of driving conditions on roads right across Western Europe. Their 'A'-plate car was one of the first to be registered in the UK and suffered from similar teething problems to those found by the *Car* trio: the ride was a little harsh for some and the ventilation system came in for some criticism. Both niggles had already been addressed by Peugeot by the time their article was published.

Tellingly, they picked up on the car's tendency to idle erratically – a characteristic which will be very familiar to owners today and which was solved by raising the idle speed above the recommended setting. The servicing costs may raise a wry smile too. Supplying dealer McKinnon of Wallington charged the princely sum of £30, which even included the cost of a set of rubber mats.

Overall, their opinions were highly positive, which was all the more remarkable given the extensive nature of the test – 25,000 miles in the space of a year was a huge amount for such a small car at the time. Not unexpectedly, the car's handling characteristics were singled out for praise: 'On twisty country roads the GTI's ability to entertain and reward is limitless,' they said, adding, 'Given these conditions it deserves six stars.'

The engine, too, was held in high regard, described as, 'Refined and eager...' and '[it] positively incites you to work it hard, using the full rev range.'

Summing up, the testers confirmed how popular the car had proved with magazine staff. Minor grumbles were always ignored whenever the opportunity to drive it arose. It was, they concluded, 'A great car with just a few detail shortcomings.'

Peugeot stated that customer feedback had been strong with most reporting high levels of satisfaction. In that first year of production, notes to dealers were issued to rectify faulty door locks and replace noisy brake callipers with modified units.

The 205 GTI was charging hard after the hot hatch competition.

CHAPTER FOUR

The Showroom Battle

In May 1984 the 205 T16 made its debut in the World Rally Championship. Finnish legend Ari Vatanen, former world champion and multiple Paris–Dakar winner, began the campaign at Corsica with Frenchman Jean-Pierre Nicolas in the co-driver's seat. Though it arrived relatively late in the season, the T16 was soon getting noticed. Vatanen drove the car to its first victory four rounds later, taking the podium at his home event, the Thousand Lakes Rally. He went on to win four of the last five rallies of the season and expectations were high for 1985. Sadly, the dangers of Group B were already becoming apparent. Italian Attilio Bettega was killed in his Lancia at Corsica and Vatanen was to suffer season-ending injuries in a horrific accident in Argentina. Vatanen's teammate and fellow Finn Timo Salanen took over. By coincidence, the next round was the Thousand Lakes and Salanen took first place. With Group B making headlines all over the world, Salanen handed Peugeot Talbot Sport their first ever World Championship.

The Group B controversy did nothing to harm sales. In 1984, after an outright win for Vatanen and co-driver Terry Harryman in the Lombard RAC Rally, Peugeot laid out the ethos behind the car in a piece of promotional literature.

'The 205 Turbo 16 was built to win international rallies, and was designed from fundamentals to achieve this objective within Group B of World Championship Rallying Regulations.' Alongside photographs of an airborne rally car and its champagne-spraying victorious crew, it continued: 'Seen on the British rally stages the 205 Turbo 16 reminds one strongly of a big brother to the 205 GTI that has been such a sales success, the rally car beating all comers with no visible effort.'

Win on Sunday, sell on Monday.

Against this backdrop, the 205 GTI began to fly out of the showrooms. Peugeot filmed a TV commercial in which a James Bond-style character raced a Cherry Red car through a mountain landscape. The plucky little GTI slid sideways across frozen lakes, dodged missiles and bombs and even leapt from a ski jump before delivering our hero to his date with a beautiful woman. Subtle it most definitely was not. Thirty years later, the company revisited the advert with a CGI-heavy short in which the 205 was replaced by its descendant, the thirtieth anniversary 208 GTI. Try as they might, the magic wasn't there.

Insanely desirable, the 205 GTI was rapidly becoming the must-have car of the day, equally at home in the car park of a country pub or outside the city centre wine bars and bistros that, in the mid-eighties, were popping up like mushrooms after a shower.

Johnny Hawkins with two 205 GTIs outside the family business in 1987. The car on the right has been fitted with a bonnet from a 205 Automatic – a popular cosmetic modification at the time.

Originally established in the small town of St Stephen in the 1940s, Hawkins Motor Group is now the oldest family-owned car dealership group in the county of Cornwall. In 1972 the company was appointed as a Peugeot main dealer and quickly opened a second garage in Hayle. Today, the company holds franchises to sell vehicles from five manufacturers, but Dealer Principal Johnny Hawkins clearly remembers the first time he set eyes on the 205 GTI.

Then a mechanic with the family firm, Johnny recalls the grey car arriving on the back of a transporter. With the instinct of one steeped in the business, he immediately knew the car was something special: 'What a looker,' was his first thought on the matter. Although the earlier 104 was, in his words, quite a good car, the 205 was a game changer. The 205 had a massive impact on both Peugeot and Hawkins as a dealership, the GTI being very much the icing on the cake.

'They weren't hard to sell,' he recalls. 'Everybody wanted one.' Demonstrators would be taken off the fleet after three months and still command full list price, such was the demand for the car.

At the start of 1987, Peugeot filmed an advert at a local clay mine featuring both 205 and 309 models. The Hawkins dealership looked after the press fleet cars during filming. As part of a wider promotion, a 205 T16 in full rally colours was displayed at the garage. For a young mechanic in his early twenties it was too much to resist. Johnny borrowed the car for an evening and remembers being stunned by its performance. He was, however, very careful to ensure filming had been completed before he took it – crashing it would have been rather awkward.

Recognising the huge contribution made to the company by the 205 GTI, they have collected several pristine, low-mileage examples and plan to open a museum to celebrate the history of the business.

Above, below and opposite above: This rally replica wearing distinctive Peugeot Sport colours was built by Hawkins Motors in the 1980s. Pictured in their compound, the car will shortly be undergoing a full restoration ahead of being exhibited in their Cornwall Museum.

Above, below and overleaf: A pair of 205 GTIs recently taken in part-exchange for new Peugeots by Hawkins Motor Group. The white car still bears its original dealer sticker in the rear window. The low-mileage cars were too good to trade and have been kept by the dealership.

By the mid-eighties, if class distinctions were beginning to become blurred in society, the same was very much true in the automotive world. It was already clear that the sands were shifting in terms of how segments were designated. Cars were getting bigger. It was becoming difficult to tell whether a model should be classed as a city car, a supermini, A-sector, B-sector, etc. During these nascent years of the hot hatchback, several models 'jumped' a class. The Golf was (and remains) a good example of this. The first iteration was a small car – the 205 was a similar size to the Mk 1 Golf – but the Mk 2 of 1983 was noticeably bigger. The Ford Fiesta, too, had grown and the Escort would soon follow in its footsteps. Vauxhall's Astra, launched in 1980, became a bigger car in 1984. Model

A 205 GTI is dwarfed between two small (by modern standards) cars, making its case as an ideal vehicle for today's busy towns and cities.

generations were not introduced at the same time; there was considerable overlap between manufacturers. Debate over which cars should be pitched against each other raged on.

The hot hatch arms race had turned into all-out war. Any manufacturer standing still would soon find themselves left behind. For 1986, Peugeot introduced a series of changes to keep the 205 GTI fresh and competitive. Cosmetically, the wing mirrors were changed for a new look more in keeping with the car's overall design. Amber side repeater indicators were added to the wings. A reworked cylinder head, larger valves and new camshaft boosted power to 115 bhp.

1986 also saw the range expanded for the first time. The fashion for open-top motoring had led to several competitors offering cabriolets based on their hatchback models. Seeing the opportunity, Peugeot turned to Pininfarina to produce an open version of the 205 and the 205 CTI, of which more later, which was unveiled in the summer.

That year, Volkswagen upped the ante by launching a range-topping sixteen-valve version of the Golf GTI. Vauxhall, too, now offered its Mk 2 Astra GTE with a 2.0 litre engine producing 124 bhp. Ford had fallen back on its rich sporting history and revised the RS name for its hottest hatch. The short-lived RS1600i made way for a 126 bhp turbocharged Escort in 1985. Painted in fashionable white and with the requisite side skirts to match, the Escort RS Turbo had a top speed of 127 mph and a fine tradition to uphold. Meanwhile, the company was readying its own Group B challenger and planned to return to the highest echelon of the sport with full factory backing. Its RS200 would, the company hoped, help it to capitalise on the marketing opportunity presented by the WRC phenomenon.

Left and below:
The older-style wing
mirror.

Above and below: The newer wing mirror fitted from 1986.

A pair of 205 CTIs.

An early 1.9 GTI.

44

Peugeot met the challenge by offering even more power. The 1.9 GTI went on sale in December. Priced at £8,445, the 1.9 GTI was given stiffer suspension, all-round disc brakes (the 1.6 used drums at the rear) and a half-leather interior. Fifteen inch alloy wheels were crammed into the arches and electric windows became a standard feature. Most important of all, the XU9JA engine had its stroke increased by 15 mm to 88 mm, raising the capacity to 1,905 cc. The 1.9 had a power output of 130 bhp at 6,000 rpm and a significantly higher torque figure (118.7 lb/ft at 4,750 rpm) than the 1.6. The crucial 0–60 time was almost two seconds quicker than the smaller-engined car, and at 7.8 seconds was well under the magical 8. Top speed was now listed at 127 mph. The 1.9 was a match for the others. It was now a straight fight.

The year drew to a close with another highly visible victory for Peugeot – the 205 T16 won its second straight World Rally Championship. Any New Year celebrations must have been very short-lived as the team clearly wasn't resting on its laurels. 1987 was ushered in with another victory. The T16 was the outright winner in January's Paris–Dakar Rally.

CHAPTER FIVE

Taking the Top Off

By the middle of the eighties the recession that had afflicted the earlier part of the decade was fading into the distance. This was the era of Reaganomics and trickledown theory. In London, the Thatcher government was about to unleash Big Bang, deregulating the financial markets. The country was starting to boom. Though the long-term effects can be (and are) debated endlessly, a lot of money was certainly sloshing around the economy. It was the decade of excess. Greed, for lack of a better (stolen) phrase, was good. Conspicuous consumption defined the age; if you've got it, flaunt it was very much the mantra. This was an ethos that was picked up by the designers of the time. It could be seen in the fashions and, of course, the cars.

Convertible motoring underwent something of a boom in the 1980s. The two-box hatchback offered the perfect opportunity for full, four-seat, rag-top cars, bringing open top motoring to the masses. Thanks to improvements in design and materials, style-conscious buyers were able to take advantage of a multitude of roofless family cars, sharing an experience that was normally reserved for two-seater sports cars.

Peugeot had form with convertibles. The elegant 504 convertible had made its world debut at the Salon de Geneva in 1969 and the 402 Eclipse *Decapotable* became the first car in the world with a retractable hard top, utilising a design patented by Georges Paulin as long ago as 1931. More recently the PSA group Talbot Samba (based on the Peugeot 104) had been available as a convertible, designed and built by Pininfarina. Recognising the potential of an open 205, Peugeot again turned to the Italian coachbuilder. It was necessary to quickly bring a car to market, one that retained the inherent good looks of the hatchback while refusing to compromise on the performance associated with the GTI.

Pininfarina went to work. The already rigid shell was stiffened by the addition of wider sills and two chassis cross members. In order to cope with so-called scuttle shake, a roll bar was added behind and above the front seats, effectively extending the B-pillars across the cabin. Although needed, the strengthening added almost 90 kg in extra weight, which had an obvious effect on performance. The convertible made use of the same 1.6 litre engine as its fixed-roof sister, but softer suspension was used to alleviate the effects of body flex.

Badged as the 205 CTI and with the coachbuilder's name proudly worn on its haunches, the new car went on UK sale in 1986. Four colours were available at the outset: White, Red, Graphite Grey and a new shade, Haze Blue. At £9,495, the CTI would cost a buyer

The 205 CTI can trace its ancestry back through a variety of vehicles, including the Talbot Samba Convertible.

A nod to the past. Though not strictly a convertible, the open Peugeot Type 26 dates back to the turn of the twentieth century. This example is displayed by the official museum *L'Aventure Peugeot*.

around £2,000 more than its tin-top equivalent. Once again, it needed to be right. Pininfarina had done a wonderful job with the styling. Whether the roof was raised or stowed away beneath its neat tonneau cover, the CTI was as pretty as any 205. It might have taken a half a second or so more to get to sixty and topped out at 'only' 118 mph, but the carefree joy of wind-in-the-hair motoring more than compensated.

Above and below: Up and down, side by side. Two 205 CTIs ably demonstrating the crisp, clean lines of the Pininfarina design whether the convertible top is raised or lowered.

During its production run, the CTI would eventually be joined by two more convertibles. In 1988, the smaller-engined CJ (Cabriolet Junior) went on sale to be followed a year later by the limited-edition Roland Garros. Contrary to popular assumption, Garros was not in fact a tennis player. In producing the Pinewood Green model with its distinctive white roof, Peugeot (like the annual Paris tennis tournament) was choosing to honour a pioneer of early aviation and *Legion d'honneur* winning First World War fighter ace. Just 150 Roland Garros Cabriolets were sold in the UK, with surviving examples sought-after collectables.

1991 marked the end of the XU5J 1.6 litre engine across the 205 range. For its last years of production, the 205 CTI was only available with the 1.9 power unit.

Any colour you want so long as it's green. The 205 Roland Garros was named in honour of the French fighter ace. Note the Pinifarina signature badge on the rear quarter and front wing Roland Garros decal.

CHAPTER SIX

Mid-life Improvements

Unlike the competition, Peugeot resisted any temptation to make the 205 a bigger car. The basic 205 bodyshell remained unchanged throughout its entire fifteen-year production run (though it should be noted that the rear wheel arches on both the GTI and CTI shells were slightly larger than normal in order to accommodate their alloy wheels). The company instead opted to make a series of gradual revisions – subtle upgrades to enhance both the interior and exterior appearance as fashions changed and customer tastes demanded.

In 1988 the 205 GTI was given a full interior makeover. A new dashboard included a reshaped instrument binnacle. Having been the source of some criticism, the centrally

Above and opposite above: Old and new instrument binnacles.

The heater controls and switchgear on an early 205 GTI. Note the vertical sliders and light grey plastic trim.

Rotary heater controls didn't just look more modern. The new design was ergonomically efficient with a more intuitive operation.

mounted heater controls were changed from rather old-fashioned sliders to more ergonomic and easier to operate rotary controls. A new three-spoke steering wheel replaced the two-spoke item and there were trim changes for both the 1.6 and 1.9 with the 'Monaco' cloth pattern replacing the older 'Biarritz'. New door cards added padding where there had previously been exposed metal to complete the up-to-date look.

In June 1989 the three millionth 205 rolled off the production line. Two months later the GTI received a bigger exhaust and new gearbox. The reverse gear selection position had never been ideal on the outgoing BE1 box. Located next to first, it was engaged with the use of a 'pull-up' collar mechanism on the stick. This led to complaints that the driver's hand would come into contact with the passenger seat while changing. The new BE3 gearbox addressed this by moving the selection to a position 'beneath' fifth. A small change, yet one which gave a much more intuitive feeling.

By this time environmental concerns were starting to come to the fore. Research had shown that the lead content in petrol was having adverse effects on health – particularly that of children. Youngsters who lived near motorways or busy town centres had been shown to have unacceptably high levels of lead in their blood and it was directly attributable to petrol. With a list of potential ailments including hypertension, brain damage, increased risk of heart

An original
two-spoke
steering wheel.
The gearstick
'collar' can be
seen at the
bottom left of
the photo (an
aftermarket
gear knob has
been fitted to
this car as the
component is
prone to failure
due to cracking
over time).

Early cars
featured
doors with
body-coloured
exposed metal.
This is the
interior of a
1987-registered
1.9 GTI with
half-leather
seats fitted as
standard.

One of the older interior trim styles. The reverse selector collar can be seen on the gear stick.

A 1991-registered 1.6 car's interior.

Half-leather interior of a 1.9 GTI. The previously exposed metal in the doors of older cars was now replaced with padded trim, giving a more luxurious feel to the cabin. Three-spoke steering wheels were now standard across the range.

attack or stroke, it was clear that something needed to be done. The government had pledged to massively reduce lead and the first unleaded pumps appeared in 1986. It was planned that Four Star fuel should be gradually phased out. In January 1989, *Autocar* magazine claimed: 'Unleaded fuel is now an inevitability – sooner or later, we will all be filling our cars with it.'

In order to be able to use unleaded it was necessary for cars to be fitted with catalytic converters. The option was first offered on the 1.9 GTI in October, albeit with a slightly adverse effect on power, which was reduced to 122 bhp.

The curtains were closing on the 1980s. The Peugeot brand had been catapulted back into the spotlight thanks to the success of Gérard Welter's visionary small car. PSA Group opted to launch its replacement for the Talbot Horizon as the Peugeot 309 (and in fact began the process of retiring the Talbot name). Built at both Poissy and the Ryton Plant close to Coventry, the 309 spawned another well-regarded GTI, although it didn't share the sharp good looks of its smaller stablemate. The plaudits continued with the 405. Entering the highly competitive saloon market in 1987, the 405 was voted European Car of the Year and became a firm fleet favourite.

1987 also heralded changes on the world rallying scene. Following a series of tragic accidents, the FIA introduced new regulations. Very sadly, the up close and personal nature of the sport had resulted in the deaths of both competitors and spectators. At a

Above, below and opposite above: Built both in France and the UK as a replacement for the Talbot Horizon, the Peugeot 309 spawned another accomplished GTI. Three and five-door variants were available. Despite the inevitably compromised looks brought about by its design brief, the car was a success with customers who wanted high performance in a larger car. The five-door car is carrying a Peugeot BMX on its roof rack – another hit for the company during the 1980s.

Above and overleaf: A handsome car from every angle, the 405 saloon went toe to toe with the Ford Sierra and Vauxhall Cavalier in the lucrative company car market. This range-topping 405 Mi-16 could back up its looks with blistering performance.

stroke the era of Group B was over. The new rules meant the cars were no longer able to compete in the World Rally Championship; in the end, they were simply too fast. Peugeot Talbot Sport instead entered the T16 into the Paris–Dakar Rally. To better cope with the punishing African terrain, the wheelbase was extended and the track widened. The car had its range extended by the addition of larger fuel tanks and the suspension was uprated. With Ari Vatanen back behind the wheel, the 205 T16 went on to win the event in 1987, 1989 and 1990.

In order to keep the 205 GTI fresh and relevant, Peugeot produced a run of limited-edition models. With their bright Miami Blue or lustrous Sorrento Green paint, the cars were certainly eye-catching. Power-assisted steering – now an option on the standard GTIs – was fitted as standard, helping to increase their appeal. Unfortunately, the appeal of the car was not restricted to legitimate owners. A new phenomenon, one that would have a devastating effect on the insurability of all hot hatchbacks, was starting to get noticed.

Above and overleaf spread: In the years 1989–90 Peugeot produced 1,200 limited edition cars in two completely new colours. Offered in either Sorrento Green or Miami Blue, there was an equal split of 600 1.6 and 600 1.9 variants. In addition to the special paint, each car was fitted with power-assisted steering, a sliding sunroof and full leather upholstery with matching grey carpets and door cards. This low-mileage example is owned by Peter Baldwin, who acquired the vehicle in 2015. Coming from a family with a history of Peugeot ownership stretching as far back as 1968, he had always wanted a 205 GTI. When this car became available, he took the opportunity and, in his own words, 'has never regretted it.'

60

Above and below: Miami Blue was a hit from the start.

From the first time he got behind the wheel of his father's 205 GR, James Hasler knew there was something very special about the car. By the early nineties he was working for a Basingstoke dealership, and was in fact the top Peugeot sales executive in Hampshire, Berkshire and Buckinghamshire. He found the 205 GTI appealed to a very wide demographic. He recalled that it was the car every enthusiast wanted to buy. The 205 GTI was everything. It was easy to drive, incredibly practical, looked brilliant and put a smile on your face. The car had a character all of its own, something you couldn't touch that made it special.

James Hasler putting a 1.6 GTI demonstrator to good use at Silverstone, sometime around 1990. Here, he fondly explains what is happening in the photo:

'There was a Peugeot GTI Club day held there and we were allowed out on the short circuit. They sent us out in batches of ten cars on the track at any one time. I was car number 8 out of the pits and we were allowed seven laps as time was getting short. I managed to get in eight as I had passed everybody by the end of the first lap and lapped the back markers before they could complete their seventh! Someone told me I was the fifth fastest car on the track that day and by far the fastest 1.6. How they knew, I don't know, but given that there were two Gutmann converted cars (a 309 and a 205 1.9) plus there was also a factory 309 GTI-16 (French market only), all with professional drivers, I was very pleased. It just goes to show that the 1.6 in the right hands is a match for a 1.9 in those less experienced! It was, of course, not my car either!'

Which Was the Better Drive, 1.6 or 1.9?

The debate has long raged among drivers of the two respective models. However, a definitive answer remains elusive and probably always will. While the larger capacity model had a higher top speed and could get there more quickly than its kid brother, it was, in many respects, a very different car to drive. The 1.6 was (and remains) a wonderfully communicative car. With its benign handling and entirely predictable mannerisms, it flattered the average driver. Taller wheels and lower-profile tyres gave the 1.9 greater levels of grip. On a track, the 1.9 would leave a 1.6 in its wake but the story could sometimes be different in real-world road conditions. Pushed too hard by an unwary driver, the 1.9 could bite. Properly exploited by an experienced driver the more powerful car would always win out, but apocryphal tales of cars heading rear-end first through hedgerows went some way to giving the 1.9 GTI a bad-boy reputation. Today, advances in tyre technology may well have calmed such tendencies but notoriety, once attained, can be very hard to shift.

Another consideration had nothing to do with how the car performed at high speed; in fact, the very opposite. Without power-assisted steering both cars were rather hard work to park. The 1.9 in particular, with its bigger wheel and tyre combination, felt especially heavy. It was not unheard of for dealers to over-inflate the tyres to compensate when demonstrating cars to unsuspecting buyers. The addition of PAS was welcomed on the 1.9 by all but out-and-out enthusiast drivers.

While both versions, of course, have their virtues and vices, it seems a solution to the eternal question may never be found.

CHAPTER SEVEN

An Ending

Car crime was starting to rapidly rise in the UK. Due to an arcane feature of the law, the act of taking a car was not punishable as theft. It was (and still is) punishable as a separate offence – taking without the owner's consent. Cars of the time were not particularly difficult to steal; little more than a screwdriver was needed. Nightly news programmes would broadcast footage of high-speed chases as performance cars were simply taken by gangs of TWOCers and used to bait the police. Joyriding became a serious problem. Insurers demanded ever-higher premiums and insisted on restrictions. The phrase 'Thatcham Approved' entered the lexicon as owners of performance cars found cover was impossible to obtain without installing all manner of anti-theft devices. Another altogether different hot hatch arms race had started, waged this time between the designers of car alarms and immobilisers and the thieves who sought to overcome them. The writing

Above and overleaf: Laser Green joined the line-up for the 1991 model year.

was on the wall, not just for the 205 GTI, but for all the other cars that had helped to bring affordable, accessible performance to the masses. It was the beginning of the end of the first hot hatchback age.

For the 1991 model year another new colour, Laser Green, was added to the paint card. July of that year saw the number of 205s produced hit an incredible 4 million. With specification becoming ever more crucial, the GTI was fitted with remote central locking, and air conditioning joined the options list for the first time.

Production of the XU5J engine ceased in September 1992 and the last of the 1.6 litre cars were sold in the UK. Final list price was £11,375. Customers buying a new 205 GTI or CTI would now have no choice, the only available engine being the catalyst equipped XU9J making 122 bhp. The decade of decadence was now but a memory and, as if reflecting this, the iconic red carpet was no more. It was replaced with a much more staid black or grey item – the GTI had grown up.

Then, late in 1992, another marketing opportunity presented itself. BBC Radio 1 was about to celebrate twenty-five years on the air. To mark the event, the station decided to team up with Peugeot to create a promotional vehicle that could be sold at a premium to raise money for a children's charity. The result was the ultra-limited-edition Peugeot 205 GTI 1FM. Arguably, the 1FM was the ultimate 205 GTI to hit the UK market. It was a fitting swansong for a car that was already well on its way to becoming a legend.

Nothing lasts forever. In 1991 Peugeot launched the 106 supermini and two years later it was followed by the 306, a direct replacement for the 309. The writing was on the wall for the 205. Production of the model would continue well into the nineties, with the last car rolling off the production line as late as 1998. For the GTI, though, time was nearly up.

Hot hatchbacks in general were no longer flavour of the month. The aforementioned wave of thefts had rendered them all incredibly expensive to insure. Premiums for younger drivers – very much a key target market – were prohibitively dear. This, coupled with the effects of an economic downturn that was starting to grip the country, sounded the death knell. Another factor in their demise may well have come from Japan. In 1989, Mazda released a car with instant appeal. With a stylistic nod to the Lotus Elan of the sixties, the MX-5 took all that was good from the classic British sports car of old and repackaged it into a thoroughly modern, safe and attractive two-seater. Most importantly, it didn't suffer from seventies build quality. The MX-5 worked. It was an immediate hit with drivers who wanted to experience the thrill of open-top motoring without the need to spend hours under the bonnet each weekend. Things had gone full circle; Mazda had brought the sports car back to life.

Sales of the 205 GTI 1.9 came to an official end in 1993 and the last new car found its owner a year later. The car that had done so much to rewrite the book on what could be expected from a small runabout hatchback was no more. It was over.

CHAPTER EIGHT

Motorsport

While we have rightly remembered the 205 T16s dominating performances at the top level of motorsport, the humble GTI, too, was making its own impact in the rally scene's less glamorous classes. That impact continues to this day, with many amateur-run 205 GTIs still competing successfully in rallies up and down the land.

Ford's rear-wheel-drive Mk 1 and 2 Escorts had dominated the sport for years, but time was moving on. The advent of the 205 GTI added a new competitor to the mix. Light, strong, compact and incredibly agile, it was an obvious choice. The little Peugeot was reliable and simple to maintain with a plentiful stock of relatively cheap motorsport parts available. By coincidence, one of the features that made the 205 such a successful road car also played a part in its success on the rally stages. The torsion bar rear suspension set up and horizontally located dampers, which gave the car its interior space, also reduced the car's tendency to understeer. Instead, the 205 GTI would, if sufficiently provoked, display oversteer characteristics similar to those of a more classic rear-drive set up. Put simply, a well-driven 205 GTI could be made to slide around the tightest of corners with incredible speed.

The name Louise Aitken-Walker needs no introduction to fans of the sport. Made an MBE in 1992, the Scottish driver was awarded the Segrave Trophy for 'Outstanding skill, courage and initiative on land, water and in the air' in 1990. It followed a decade of success, which culminated in her taking the Ladies' World Rally Title the same year. Throughout her fourteen-year career she took the wheel of numerous iconic rally cars, but it was in 1985 that she first strapped herself into a 205 GTI with Peugeot Talbot Sport UK. In her own words, 'It was a match made in heaven.'

At first, she found the car didn't 'ride the bumps' very well. It had a tendency to bounce on landing after a jump, making it a little unpredictable. Louise, who is still involved with setting up rally cars today, asked the Coventry-based engineers to give the car a slightly different suspension set-up. It wasn't a drastic change – just a different sized rear torsion bar – but it made a world of difference. From then on, she knew nobody could touch her in the little Peugeot. She knew she was going to set the world alight. 'I loved it,' she said, enthusing about her two seasons in the car, 'it suited me down to the ground.'

It was, she said, one of those magic years, remembering how much fun she had. Up against an incredibly competitive field, people were baffled by how fast she could make the 205 GTI go. In the 1987 season she took five out of five wins in the British Open Rally

Championship: 'A right good battle; a great team effort.' It was a performance that led to her being voted *Autosport* magazine's Driver of the Year.

Her proudest achievement with the car would come in the 1988 WRC Mintex Rally. On paper the car was an underdog, going into battle against more powerful, all-wheel drive opposition. Delighting supporters all over the land, Louise and co-driver Ellen Walker rode a wave of popularity and stormed to second place overall. The 205 GTI was writing the headlines again.

Things, however, didn't always go exactly to plan. On one memorable occasion she was attacking a stage in the Isle of Man. Mishearing a pace note, she lost control of the car and ended up heading the wrong way down a narrow lane. The car, which had been 'flying down the stage' crashed straight through a high hawthorn hedge and came to an unceremonious halt in the middle of a private garden. The householder appeared, an irate elderly gentleman. Both driver and co-driver apologised profusely for the error but nothing they said could calm him down. When they were eventually able to get away, the humour of the situation hit and neither of them could stop laughing. For many years afterwards the 'Hole in the Hedge' brought a wry smile to Louise's face whenever she passed along the route. Louise's enthusiasm for the Peugeot still shines through. 'It was a fantastic car,' she recalls. Her answer, when asked what made it so special, came without hesitation: 'Four wheels right on the corners. No overhangs – a little go-kart.'

Despite being phased out nearly two decades ago, the 205 GTI is still a regular sight on the club rally circuit today.

Above and pages 70–72: A selection of photos showing 205 GTIs in action at the Prescott Hill Climb, Gloucestershire.

Above and below: Pierre Newton in his 205 GTI tarmac rally car.

CHAPTER NINE

Resurgence

As the new millennium began to get into its stride, the 205 GTI cut a rather sad figure on the roads. An analogue solution in an increasingly digital world, shabby examples started to appear in the bargain basement listings. These were the *Max Power* magazine years. The cruising scene took off across the UK and all manner of cars were subjected to all manner of modifications. By now very cheaply available, the 205 GTI became one of the prime candidates to be adorned with unfortunate body kits, oversized wheels and extensive in-car entertainment systems. The advent of another phenomenon – the track day – saw yet more cars converted to circuit use.

Although essentially mechanically robust, high mileages took their toll and, inevitably, original engines began to wear out. Replacements were sought. In what now seems an act of sacrilege, one particular upgrade involved transplanting the sixteen-valve 1.9 litre engine from Peugeot's short-lived 405 Mi-16 saloon. Another popular donor was the 306 2.0 GTI-6. Clean, original 205 GTIs started to disappear from sight. For an erstwhile automotive giant, it looked to be an ignominious end.

But then something happened. Although they certainly declined in popularity, hot hatchbacks never completely went away. The new breed was, however, often compromised – their performance blunted by the need to add size and weight in line with the demands of the modern consumer. With each new launch, the same question was asked in the magazines, the TV programmes and, increasingly, the websites that were rapidly changing the media: could this one be the new 205 GTI? The answer, invariably, was no.

Peugeot brought the GTI badge out of retirement in 1996 for the 106 supermini. It was a very good car. For all the reasons outlined earlier, its more muted appearance didn't advertise its sporting intentions with the brash confidence of the 205 and it never quite caught the same level of public attention. In 1998, the 205 was perhaps more directly replaced by the 206. The model would eventually become Peugeot's biggest ever sales success. A GTI was added to the UK range five years later. Accomplished though the new model was, it could never match its predecessor's tantalising combination of light weight, raw energy and sheer driveability. In fairness to Peugeot, no other manufacturer had managed to do so either. The 205 GTI was taking on a mythical status.

It is nigh-on impossible to predict which of the myriad cars released onto the world's markets will attain classic status. Low-volume, high-priced exotica are usually guaranteed their place among the stars but for a lowly, mass-market runabout, something rather special is needed. Sporting prowess helps, as many Ford models have, over the years, ably proved. Success on the racetrack or rally circuit is not, however, any guarantee of survival. To gain, as it were, a second life, a car needs to capture the imagination of the public, to invoke nostalgia, to make people point and smile.

In researching and writing this book it has become very clear that the 205 GTI has a very rosy future indeed. A plethora of businesses are now producing all manner of equipment for the 205 GTI, for both motorsport and road use. Over the last three and a half decades a wealth of expert knowledge has been gathered together, enabling owners to get the best from their cars and keep them in tip-top condition. Thanks to its robust engine and galvanised body, a looked-after 205 will give years of good service and cover incredibly high mileages. Solutions to many of the problems that have manifested themselves have been found. Surprising information is shared through the owners' network – who ever would have thought that a prone-to-failure coin tray catch could be replaced for pennies with an identical item fitted to Brabantia bread bins? Peugeot themselves have recognised the love that exists for their creation and begun to remanufacture and supply a large inventory of spares. Their *L'Aventure Peugeot* museum service has thousands of products available through a comprehensive website.

Shorn of the unfair hooligan image it gained through the hard years of the 1990s, the 205 GTI has enjoyed something of a mainstream resurgence. Many are being reclaimed, with modifications being removed and cars restored to standard condition. Against a backdrop of cars that are more like kitchen appliances – amorphous blobs sold on their 'connectivity' rather than performance – the sight of a 205 GTI out on the road rarely fails to make someone smile. For their drivers, there is very much a feeling of cheating the system. Thanks in part to their diminutive size, they are now the perfect city car, capable of nipping through the densest traffic and parking in the smallest spaces.

A thriving club scene exists. Originally founded as the Peugeot 205 GTI Club by the manufacturer itself, what is today called the Peugeot Sport Club retains official status and enjoys strong links with the company. The club has an active membership and a number of well-supported affiliated local groups. Touring and motorsport events are organised and every summer the annual Pugfest festival attracts visitors from all around the country and abroad.

Perhaps in contrast with some other classic car clubs, there is a broad membership demographic. There is no typical member. Those who drive Peugeot 205 GTIs share a common bond – a special secret they have all discovered and which keeps them from becoming disillusioned with the parlous state of motoring in the UK today.

We know we'll never own the fastest car in the world. Even for those of us lucky enough to have the very latest hypercar of the moment in the garage, any glory will only be short-lived. There will always be another ultra-low volume manufacturer closing fast behind, someone else chasing that unattainable goal with a crated F1 engine bolted to an improbable, ground-hugging monster of a two-seat monocoque. And for what? The main roads, certainly in the UK, become more and more congested every day. What passes for an acceptable surface more often than not resembles the Sea of Tranquility. Speed limits are policed more stringently than ever; make the slightest of transgressions and a camera, somewhere, will get you.

Above, below and opposite: Peugeot 205 GTIs en masse at the annual Peugeot Sport Club event, Pugfest. Members from all around the country and abroad gather to admire the cars.

Thankfully, for the 205 GTI driver, things are not as joyless as they seem. There are still, believe it or not, satisfying strips of tarmac to be found. Go somewhere far away from the crowds. Find a quiet B road. Sit behind that thin-rimmed wheel and turn the little plastic key. Listen to the starter spin, kickstarting its eager little four-cylinder heart. The lion rampant once again. Take a moment to hear the familiar, splattery crackle from the exhaust just behind you. Then, as the tickover (hopefully) settles, try not to smile as you ease the 205 GTI into gear and head on out onto the open road.

Above: Seen here at the Rockingham Circuit, this 205 GTI 1.6 is owned by Chris Hughes, Marketing Manager for Peugeot Sport Club UK.

Left: A regular exhibitor at classic car shows, Chris has owned his 205 GTI for nearly twenty years.

The well-travelled car has been all over France. Here it sits atop the Col de l'Iseran, at 2,764 metres (9,068 feet) the highest mountain pass in France.

Above and overleaf: When Ben Robertson bought his 1.9 GTI on eBay, he didn't quite realise what he was getting in to. The car, which arrived on the back of a transporter, now leads a pampered life, venturing out for track days around ten times each year. Once used as his daily driver, it has achieved a ten-minute lap of the Nurburgring and been exhibited at Goodwood. By his own admission, Ben loves the car – he even refused to move house unless there was a garage for his GTI.

CHAPTER TEN

The Special Editions

1FM

The ultimate 205 GTI? In 1992, Peugeot entered into a collaboration with BBC Radio 1. Their aim was to produce a car that would capture the spirit of the station as it celebrated twenty-five years since its first ever broadcast. Just twenty-five cars were produced, making the 1FM one of the rarest 205s in existence and guaranteeing exclusivity for a handful of lucky owners. Their specification was highly impressive for the time. 1FM models had anti-lock brakes, sliding sunroofs, remote central locking, full leather trim and – rather tellingly – engine immobilisers as standard. The jack was relocated from its normal under-bonnet location and placed beneath the front passenger seat. This made way for an air-conditioning system – back then a real rarity for a small car. In keeping with the musical theme, a high-quality sound system was fitted.

The Peugeot 205 GTI 1FM

Clarion provided a remote-control radio CD unit with an amplifier mounted behind the centre console. The parcel shelf made way for a specially produced MDF speaker shelf and a six-disc CD changer was located in the boot.

All of the 1.9 litre cars were finished in black and given anthracite-coloured Speedline wheels with polished aluminium edges (as fitted to the European-market Griffe). At the rear, the plastic trim panel was removed, the tailgate instead painted in the same high-gloss black as the rest of the bodywork. Unique 1FM badging was applied to the tailgate

Above: 1FM side decal.

Left: 1FM rear badge. Note the smooth tailgate painted in body colour.

and wings. Inside, the black leather was complemented by green stitching, grey carpets and 1FM mats. A numbered brass panel was located on the edge of the driver's door.

Ahead of their release, the cars were heavily promoted on the radio station. One was given away as a competition prize. The remaining twenty-four cars were priced at £17,000. The cost – a substantial premium over the standard 205 GTI – included a donation to the

Some of the surviving 205 GTI 1FM limited edition cars. Always a big draw at club events.

Above and overleaf: The plate tells the story. An L-registered Peugeot 205 GTI 1 FM.

Nordoff-Robbins music therapy charity, which had recently opened its centre in Kentish Town, London. Prized by their owners, the 1FM remains much sought after by collectors. A register exists to track surviving cars.

Griffe

Making its debut at the Paris Motor Show in October 1990, the Griffe was a luxurious limited edition for the mainland European market. Painted in Fluorite Green, the same colour as Jean Todt's personal 205 GTI, the 1.9 litre cars were given a very high specification. Hurricane Grey leather upholstery was finished with green stitching, as was the steering wheel and gear stick gaiter. The gear knob was printed in green, in contrast to the standard red. The Griffe sat on distinctive Speedline wheels, anthracite grey with a rim edged in brushed aluminium. Green bumper and trim inserts replaced the usual red and Griffe badging completed the exterior look. All of the cars were fitted with anti-lock brakes, power-assisted steering and a sunroof.

One thousand cars went on sale in France with a price of 112,000 Francs. A further 2,000 were exported to Germany and the Netherlands. The name reflected Peugeot's by now well-known lion theme. The word 'griffe' is French for 'claw'.

Today, Griffes are highly sought-after classics commanding large prices on the rare occasions they come up for sale.

Above, below and overleaf spread: This lovely 205 GTI Griffe is owned by Romuald Sainthérand, Secretary of the 205 GTI Club de France, who kindly supplied photos of his car.

Automatic

In 1992 a batch of 205 GTIs with four-speed automatic transmissions was produced for the Japanese market. For reasons lost in the mists of time, the order was cancelled at the last minute and the cars, being right-hand drive, were shipped all the way back from East Asia to the UK. A mix of both GTI and CTI, the 'K'-plate cars were equipped with air conditioning, power-assisted steering, heated door mirrors and sunroofs (hatchback). The cars were marketed and sold predominantly in south-east England – where the UK's market for automatic gearboxes was historically strongest. Several cars are known to still be in existence. The Peugeot 205 Gentry essentially replaced the automatics in 1993. That model had similar styling to the GTI but with its detuned engine and 'softer' track control arm front suspension, many do not consider it to be a 'proper' GTI.

Le Mans

Peugeot built eighty-four Le Mans edition 1.9 205 GTIs for sale in Sweden in 1991. All were finished in Miami Blue and fitted with a red reflective rear trim panel made by German automotive company Hella. The Le Mans had several innovations to cope with the sub-zero Scandinavian conditions to which it would be exposed. An auxiliary pre-heater was fitted to the inlet manifold to assist with cold weather starting and the front inner wings were protected by plastic guards. A headlamp wash system was plumbed into the front bumper and there was extra rust-proofing for the sills. Automatic headlamps were operated on start-up. Inside, the car had a wooden steering wheel and gear knob and heated front seats. The look was completed with a sunroof and Le Mans badging.

Conversions

Given the success of the 205 GTI, it was inevitable that many companies would offer a variety of packages to modify the style and/or enhance its performance. Some notable examples are listed below.

Gutmann

German tuning company Gutmann set out to substantially increase power over the standard GTI. They achieved this by fitting the sixteen-valve cylinder head as fitted to the 309 GTI 16v. By remapping the engine and adding an oil cooler, redesigned exhaust and a less restrictive air filter, they managed to raise the output of the 1.9 litre car from 130 PS to 160 PS. Gutmann fitted a front strut brace to increase stiffness and lowered the suspension by a hefty 30 mm (1.2 in.). A reinforced clutch and brake discs helped to rein in the increase in power. As well as their ground-hugging stance, Gutmann cars were recognisable by subtle badging as well as minor interior tweaks.

The iconic Gutmann badge on the rear of a 205 GTI modified by the company.

Interior design features of a Gutmann car.

Turbo Technics

Northampton company Turbo Technics was one of the best-known UK turbocharger companies. Their conversion made use of a Garrett T25 turbo and increased power output for both the 1.6 and 1.9 versions. Air was drawn in through the standard air filter before being passed through an intercooler mounted at the front of the engine. The result was a top speed of more than 130 mph and a 0–60 figure of less than seven seconds. By retaining the standard injection system, the company claimed that fuel consumption was unaffected during normal throttle use. Unusually for an aftermarket tuning company, Turbo Technics were so confident of their workmanship that they provided a full twelve-month mechanical breakdown warranty with an option for customers to extend. In other words, as it said in their advertising at the time, there are no worries for fortunate owners.

Dimma Designs

By 1984 the roar of the lion could be heard right across Europe. In Wandre, a suburb on the outskirts of Liege, Belgium, a Monsieur Baudoin Michel heard it too. M. Baudoin had worked in the motor industry for several years, in fact beginning his career at the Seneffe plant – British Leyland's only facility outside of the UK. His company, Dimma Designs, was founded in 1983. Perhaps taking inspiration from both the 205 T16 and another widely praised automotive design – the flamboyantly styled Ferrari Testarossa of 1984 – Dimma designed and built a wide-bodied kit for the 205. Mimicking the Italian supercar's side strakes, the Dimma 205 GTI was a real presence on the road. Shorn of the restrictions imposed by the Peugeot paint list, several wildly coloured examples were produced, with the only limits being the customer's imagination. According to the company website, Jean Todt was very much a fan of the kit. Dimma Designs would go on to modify another Peugeot model, creating a body kit for the 306 model in 1993. With rekindled interest in the 205 GTI, Dimma restarted production of their kit, now known as the Signature Series.

Dimma Designs. A GTI and CTI wearing Dimma wide-bodied kits sit side by side.

Above, below and overleaf above: The full extent of the Dimma body modifications. This pristine example is owned by Koen Marcelis.

A Dimma 205 in the workshop alongside an older brother, a rare Peugeot 505 V6 saloon.

One of these cars is giving the other a jump start.

Above and overleaf above: Two photos from the same angle show the author's car before and after restoration.

Out on the road. The author's car in its natural environment.

A pair of icons, both born in the heat of the Cold War.

Acknowledgements

By necessity a project such as this one will always rely on others. I am grateful to the many who have shared their knowledge, anecdotes and experience, giving me their time and patiently answering my almost never-ending questions.

Particular thanks go to the following. If I have overlooked anyone please accept my apologies and be assured I could not have written this book without you. It goes without saying that any mistakes are mine and mine alone.

Dan and Meirion, for working miracles on a very poorly car.

All at the Peugeot Sport Club UK, especially Chris Hughes who kindly provided me with several points of contact.

Donna Freeman and Colin Overland at Bauer Media Group for helping secure the permission to extensively quote *Car* magazine's 1984 road test article.

The Peugeot UK Press Office.

Louise and Graham Aitken-Walker.

Ian Kirkwood, for answering countless no-doubt foolish questions with the patience of a saint.

James Hasler for his invaluable insights and memories of selling and driving the 205 GTI.

Johnny Hawkins and Jeremy Philips of Hawkins Motor Group in Cornwall, both of whom were most helpful from the very outset.

Jonathan Miller, Pierre Newton, Ben Robertson, Koen Marcelis and Peter Baldwin, who all supplied me with much-needed images.

Monsieur Romuald Sainthérand, Secretary of the 205 GTI Club de France. *Merci*, Romuald.

Rachel Royer, for taking the time to find some wonderful photographs of the late Gérard Welter. *Merci pour tout*, Rachel.

Thank you, as ever, to the long-suffering Amanda for putting up with my car nonsense and to Ralf for the de-stressing walks.